A BODY OF WATER

*a collection of poetry
and other writings*

by Wadiz

First published in 2009
by A. Moon & Son Publishing

All rights reserved.
Copyright ©Wadiz 2009

The author gratefully acknowledges permission to include the work of the featured artists and illustrators.

The moral right of the author has been asserted.

This book is sold subect to the condition that it shall not, by way of trade or otherwise, be lent, resold, hired out or otherwise circulated without the publisher's prior consent in any form of binding or cover other than that in which it is published, and without a subsequent condition including this condition being placed upon the subsequent publisher.

ISBN 978-0-9562155-0-5

for Moon & Mishka

CONTENTS

Contents v
Foreword xi
Extract from *The Revellers* xiii

BEGINNING

You And I 3
The Morning Skies 4
Morning Prayer Of Thanks For The Supreme Gift.. 5
A Body Of Water 6
A Present Of Infinity In A Finite Thing
  or, A Poem For My Children. 8
This Is Where Death Lives 10
The River Mirror 12
A Red And Yellow Autumn Leaf
  On The Kitchen Table Speaks To Me 14
We Shall Feast. 16

A VERY BRIEF SELECTION OF CONFLICTS

Just Another Protest Song. 21
Two Brothers 24
Death, Would You Mind?.. 25
The Next Guy.. 27
The Girl And The Boy Soldier 28

A FEW COMEDIES

Dramatis Personæ. 33
From Whom. 34
The Four Truths.. 34
Self Taught 37
A Seed In The Soil Slowly Explodes.. 37

Finding Yourself. 37
I Was Still Enough To Notice Anyway 38
Letter To Mr S. Irwin 39
Interview With General Stoppe.. 40
Letter To The Editor Of The T —. 43
A Discursive Philosophy 44
Letter To The Editor. 50
Chaque Jour 50
A Provocative Cellist 50
Concert Review.. 51
Come Again? 53

SOME SONGS WITHOUT THEIR NOTES

Coulda Been A Buddha.. 57
A Song For Julian's 50th Birthday 58
A Dumb Song.. 62
Acoustic/Electric Christmas Song 64
Garden Gnome Choices. 65
I Always Know What You're Thinking 66
O Chooser! 68
It Was Very Good 69
Nothin' Blues 70
Gospel Song. 71

MORE INNOCENCE & EXPERIENCE

Messages From God 75
Strawberries And Champagne. 76
Under The Sea. 77
There Was A Big Fish In The Sea 77
A Student Of Goethe 78
Jack Shepherd 78
Literary Alien 78
The Wishful-Thinking Jungle Song. 80
Hungry Choices 80
No Nursery Rhyme 81

Observed	82
Both Good	82
In My Spa	82
The Uneducated Baroness	84
Lots Of Tea	84
A Moral Tale Of Reading While Eating	84
A Career In Politics	86
Santa Claus Defiant	86
Shout, Hooray!	86
Proud	88
The Duke Who Went Too Far	88
On The Virtue Of Being Polite	88
What Gavin Ate	89
My Lanky Donkey	90
O, Most Beautiful Gnat!	91
Foul Habits	92
Riddled And Diddled	92
No Rhyme	92
I Loved My Car	94
'Tis The Season	95
Frigid Maureen	96
Sorrowful Peter's Tale	97
A Lover In Fife	98
No Puck	100
Nice Can't Always Be Nice	100
A Holiday Romance	100
Be Quiet	102
A Conclusion	104
A Tardy Bus Driver	104
A Fellow's Cabinet	104
A Bright Little Thing	105
The Money Tree	105
A Staunch Vegetarian Boy	106
The Wolf-Man	107

ACHING HEARTS

What Matters In This Relationship .. .. .111
My Love Balloon.. .. .. .112
Without Your Lights. .. .. .113
My Love Is Leaving. .. .. .114
Do Not Read These Words .. .. .115
The Tall Young Man. .. .. .116
Adrift .. .. .117
Willy-Willy Dong! .. .. .117
I Am Free Now .. .. .118
ATOMBENOUGHTIMEANDERANGEL.. .. .. .118
I Could Tell You Something About Stravinsky.. 119
I Want To Do Something Else. .. .. .120
One Of The Voices .. .. .121

ENDING

Deep Joy. .. .. .125
As You Walk .. .. .126
Writer's Block. .. .. .127
A Prayer For Today's Truth-Seekers .. .. .128
We Are Here. .. .. .129
My Goodbyes (May God Be With You) .. .. .130

Afterword.. .. .. .134
Artists.. .. .. .136
Donations.. .. .. .141

Foreword

Picking up any book for the first time, I habitually skip the Foreword, sometimes never read it (unless a chance glance shows that it's short) but it's the Afterwords that always really annoy me, because, even if I want the book to end, I haven't yet been able to resist the implicit promise of fulfilment, finality and revelation, that the Last Page inevitably represents, and in my personal literary experience so far, no Afterword has been worth the candle, this present example included, so my advice to you, dear reader, is to read and take heed of this forewarning and review your behaviour and expectations appropriately.

Won't comment on the rest of the book until I have read it.

Schody Mosień
Emeritus Professor of Neuro-Science
Legris University
April 2009

Diogenes: My heart is heavy with sadness yet my blood is hot with rage, such a conflict in my breast! That it can be so is a curse of the gods who made this mortal frame!

Astaria: Gently, dear Diogenes, soften your heart, your blood may be hot but it must flow there.

Diogenes: The heat of my desire for this woman I cannot have is consuming me! I am cursed! This ever-growing weight of grief is pulling me down, I cannot bear it! I see my open grave!

Astaria: Lie down here Diogenes, lay your head in my lap, no more fighting against yourself. See, the dark cloud is passing. Let all that you already have and love return to your clearing view.

from *The Revellers*, II. iv. 20 – 32
Aescyllus (66 – 12BC)

Beginning

You And I

You, the Bright Flame,
I, the Moth,

Oh! You burn so brightly!

The Morning Skies

The horizon sighs
With pleasure
In the sunrise,
The morning skies
Light up!

Delighting in
Inviting in
Love! Life!

All is new!
Me! You!

Morning Prayer Of Thanks
For The Supreme Gift

Great Spirit of Love in all Creation,
Thank You for my sleep and dreams last night,
I am awakening now.

Thank You for this new day
And for the grace of being alive this morning.
Thank You for the miracle of creation
And for the supreme gift of this Life.

Opening to Love, I let truth and joy
Into my heart and into the hearts of others.
My Life is made of these days;
This day is made of these moments;
This moment now is my Life.

This moment is full of mystery and the unknown,
This moment is full of beauty and Love,
Let it be that I am fully alive to it all.

All I feel, all I think,
All I say, all I do and all I am
Is in harmony with You,
Great Spirit living within me,
Great Spirit I am living within,
Maker of the stars, trees and birds.

Great Spirit, thank You.

A few lines adapted from traditional prayers.

A Body Of Water

A rain drop,
a pearl fruit under this green leaf's tip,
curling inside it the earth – the horizon –
swells in my gazing,
seeps into my blood.

How the stars ride round the night sky
   till the dawn drinks them in!

O my sisters and brothers!
On the banks of this river we can waver no longer,
we have only to answer the call of the ocean,
to enter the water,
our bodies to carry our hearts in the flow.
True love has a mirror to reveal what we know,
wherever love leads me I gladly will go.

How the earth is parted
   by the seedlings' yearning push!

In springtime I'm dancing, spinning you round me,
laughing and smiling and loving you dearly,
I glow when you're near me, alive in my heart.

I have lain down in Eden and with God I've spoken,
His answers are growing wherever I look
with the eyes of a baby, a sage and a mother's son;
my breath is communion, my heartbeat a song.

In summer celebration of the ripening time,
hiding and revealing, in sacred signs,
the mysteries that ring unheard,
we rise in songs that have no words.

In autumn we walked round the garden,
the fallen leaves lay spent in damp, dark waves.
The crocuses shone beautifully at dusk.

I spent winter in firelight with you in my arms,
through the quick-to-darken days,
when the wind is old and grey
and the nights all split by frost.

Our family draws close and strong,
we each learn where we belong,
the songs we sing are the lives we lead
and the friends we need.

At solstices and festivals, whisperings with death,
we feel the seasons treading round the sun.
Here and there the children play,
and then are gone.

Snow slides off the roof.

The melting swells the river and the pond.

A Present Of Infinity In A Finite Thing, or, A Poem For My Children

Once,
Dad gave me
A fine clay pot that he'd made,
With a well-fitted lid,
And inside
Was some wrapping-paper.

I hadn't asked for anything,
And quite liked it,
But I wasn't sure
If it was a gentle joke,
Or a spiritual lesson,
Or if I was meant to do something with it.
Or, knowing Dad, probably all three.
And some more I couldn't see!

So I asked him,
And, I think, he just smiled.
And gradually
It dawned on me
That the pot had magical properties,
Of course!
In time, I discovered a few,
Ones that Dad knew,
But with these few,
Somehow I made more,
Completely new,
And they made me.

And then I saw
Dad knew this would happen too,
Yet still he was glad it had.
And I felt glad,
As never before!

Later on, I saw him again, in the garden,
Tending to the plants and earth,
And went out to join him,
Not thinking at all
But feeling so fully
All my doubts forgotten.

And my pot,
In the house,
Wrapped up.

This Is Where Death Lives (to Agata)

Openness is here before me,
Deep power and mystery,
May I drink the juice of the fruit of All!

This great treasure found now life springs!
This neck, these ears, these cheeks, these eyelids,
this nose, this mouth, these lips, this tongue,
these shoulders, elbows, wrists,
hands, fingers and fingertips,
this back this chest these breasts this belly
these hips and buttocks, this mound these lips
these thighs knees shins ankles feet and toes,

opening fulfilled in opening,
fulfilment complete in being itself,
lovers together, rising and falling,
skin and breath, heating and cooling,
joining to make one, joining to make love,
loving to make love,
bringing each to the other
to bring each to themselves,
one self in each other,

reaching one openness,
reaching one togetherness,
touching the peak of this moment of love-death-life,
this is the time of love,
this is the passion of living,
this is the oneness of the heart-body,
this is the unity of the generations before
and to come,
all time is nothing but this
and this is full of all time,
this is fullness,

this is fullness,
this is where death lives,
this is where death lives to be loved,
to be embraced,
to be fully wanted,
to be opened and entered,

death opened and entered and fully loved,
fully loved, all is released, all is given up,
all is surrendered to the ecstatic truth of
this love-death-life always loving-dying-living.

The River Mirror

Seeing the sky in the river mirror,
Flowing reflection in my eyes,
Through my body, in my blood,

Clear water flowing,
Green weed growing,
Beneath this wooden bridge.

The surface
Of the water – of the air –
To reach out and touch!

Where am I?

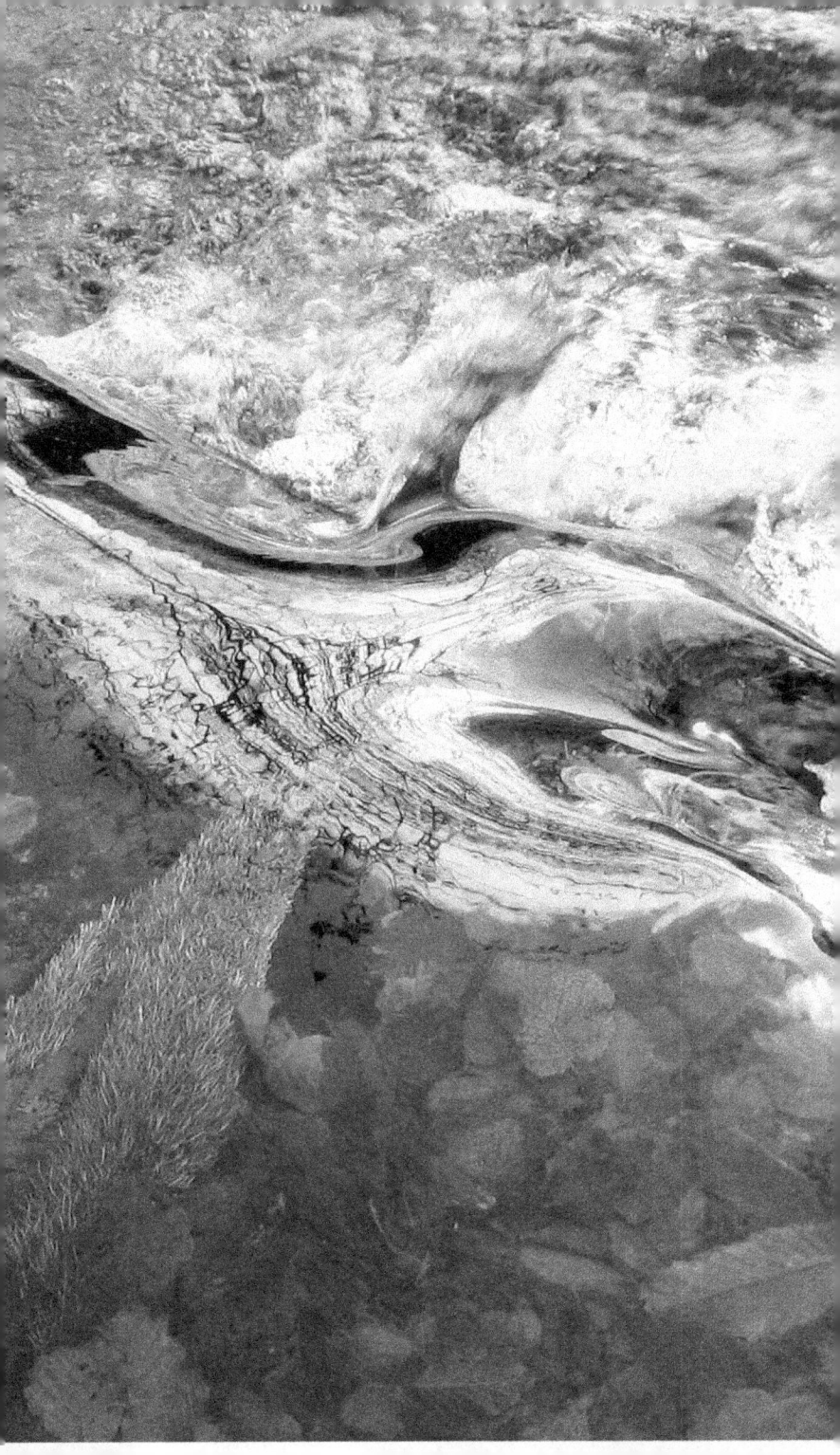

A Red and Yellow Autumn Leaf
On The Kitchen Table Speaks To Me

I am one leaf,
from one twig, one branch, one tree.
When was I more beautiful?
At no time.

You say there was a time
before I was a leaf
but what do I know of that?
You say there will be times
after I have ceased to be a leaf
but what can I know of them?

If you like, I can tell you stories:
of the swelling of the russet bud,
of springing into green fullness,
of hanging in the curled heat of midsummer,
of living within the winds in fury
and the dark, plummeting rains;
of withering, of falling,
and of touching the earth;

and still
all the stories begin and end here,
where you're asking me
how to land more deeply in your heart!

What can a fallen leaf know of that?

(to All You Fallen Leaves)

We Shall Feast

We shall feast in our secret place in the forest,
We shall incline tulip petals to our lips,
Onto our tongues the dew bead jewels glide . . .

We shall perform the ritual circle dance
around green-flame fires of sun-dried birch-bark,

We shall abandon ourselves
beneath the unblinking moonshine
of the darkhood sky,

We shall fashion our own transformations
inside birdsong and mothswings . . .

Soaring and rolling above the clouds,
Merging with flowing ecstasies,
Accepting all opening . . .

A Very Brief Selection of Conflicts

Just Another Protest Song

(transcript of the introduction to a live recording,
Sandwell Manor, June 6th 2007)

Howdy folks! Mah name's Texas Joe, sure is a pleasure to be here tonight, this is a beautiful thing happenin' right here, a beautiful thing.

Ah'm a little jet-lagged, just in from the good ol' US of A. Yeah, some fellah hasn't showed up, 'n just a few minutes ago Faith aksed me would ah fill in here, kinda last minute thing, and ah replied, happy to oblige, happy to oblige!

Ah got a song to sing for you'all, but ah ain't a singer, ah'm a soldier, jus' to warn yer. Ha! Anyways, so, ah done a real load o' travellin' aroun' past few weeks, now this is England, right? 2007? That's what you'all believe, ain't that right?

OK, so ah'm agonna ask you sumthin': ah want you'all to believe that ah'm just a country boy from Texas, an Iraqi bullet stuck in my left shoulder, and mah Southern accent is totally convincing! Sure it is!

Anyways, some o' you good people may recall the time $4\frac{1}{2}$ years [ago] the great US victory in Iraq. So ah wrote this song $4\frac{1}{2}$ years ago, and boy, was ah naive! Ah gotta tell yer, ah thought, this song is hot, you know, ah thought, this song is so hot, this song is gonna stop the war!

So ah'm gonna sing this song on condition, *on condition,* that we all agree it's up t'us to stop this war, and all wars.

Heck, why not go the whole hog, OK? Well.

OK.

So, just for a while then, at least just *act* like you give a damn, OK?

OK then, here's the song, goes sumthin' like this –

> I don' know how this started,
> or when it's gonna stop,
> I left those decisions
> to the people at the top.
> I don' know what I'm doin',
> if it's right or wrong,
> But darling, I do love you,
> that's why I wrote this song.
>
> Worked hard for this uniform,
> just like my daddy done,
> I believed to be a man
> I had to have a gun.
> *Apocalypse Now's* my favourite film,
> I got it on DVD,
> If only you were out here too,
> you could watch it here with me.

Lord, I was so willing
to make myself look good,
Which led up to me killing
because I thought I should.
I wonder who's behind all this,
what do they really want?
Does anybody understand,
'cos sure as hell, I don't.

Livin's suddenly a nightmare
of chaos, death and pain,
Only one thing now is clear:
I've joined the ranks of the insane.
If clearing up this awful mess
was truly to begin today,
Would you know just what to do
or look the other way?

I wish I was at home now,
'stead of lyin' in this sand,
My friend's dead, my leg's half off,
there's blood on my hands.
I had no idea
life could be like this,
Now nothin' feels so far away
as peace and happiness.

Who was that dead body?
Now I'll never know.
He'll never kiss his sweetheart
or watch his children grow.
Why have I thrown this life away,
this poor mother's son?

Oh, my dear children,
don't you do what I have done.

A song is entertainment
but what's this comin' along?
Just another day, just another war,
just another protest song.
One song can't make much difference,
what can one song do?
The only difference it can make
is the difference made by you.

I don' know how this started,
or when it's gonna stop,
I left those decisions
to the people at the top.
I don' know what I'm doin',
if it's wrong or right.
Have I ever really loved you?
I'm wonderin' day and night.

Can you really love me now?
I can only hope you might.

Two Brothers

There once was a shepherd named Cain
Whose heart suffered such grievous pain –
A jealous seed sown there,
A monster had grown there,
And now his own brother lay slain.

Death, Would You Mind?

(Dialogues with Self, Death and Brother.)

S: Death, would you mind having a little chat with me? Death?

D: I'm here, you don't need to call out. What can I tell you? You must know that I am always within arm's reach.

S: Yes, but where do you take me?

D: You will know, when it is your time.

S: What do I have to fear?

D: Anything you choose.

S: You seem a little, er, anti-social.

D: So you'd like to get to know me better?

S: Yes – that is, no! I meant, yes, I see what you mean, I'm not ready to leave life yet. So everything on the other side of The Styx is secret, hidden from me? I couldn't go there and then return?

D: That would be unusual.

S: O, Death! You're not much at conversation! Thank you though, for your time. I'm going to look for my dead brother and see what he can tell me. Thank you Death, goodbye!

D: See you later.

S: My brother, would you come and talk to me?

B: I'm here.

S: Oh, thank you for coming. How are you?

B: Yeah, I'm okay.

S: You sound a little flat, I thought all of you on that side were, you know, untroubled?

B: That's what you thought, is it? That it's a nice little paradise, where everyone's kind and fulfilled?

S: Well, yes, I'm, er, a bit taken aback by your tone.

B: You want me to be another in your entourage of ethereal friends, the heavenly fan club, the angelic support group? Forget it! You've got plenty of them already, you don't need me in there too. Do you know what it's like here? No. Do I know what it's like here? Yes! And when I look at you, do I feel a warm glow, a welling of pride in my young brother? No, I don't. So there you have it. Of course you have your story, everyone has their story, but you tell yours so much I'm sick of hearing it and I wish with all that's true that you were too! Just do one thing for me, my brother, just live a little, won't you please? There are those of us who don't have what you have and who would swap places with you in a flash. Understand?

S: 	Yes my brother, thank you.

The Next Guy

> *" The next guy tries to make a cunt oot o' me,*
> *ah'm warning yuz, ah'm gonna set aboot 'im! "*

So said Gordon on several occasions, though it always sounded a sadly hollow threat.

Many men in their twenties who've not yet had an emotionally engaged sexual relationship with a woman, will be carrying a more or less repressed fear that they might be gay; a fear which will inevitably be fed, unconsciously, by other young men in the same predicament.

It is surely impossible for such men to form any close friendships.

Left unchecked, the natural outcome of this fear is knife violence, one man stabbing another, perhaps to death.

The Girl And The Boy Soldier

'Where is your mother?'
Kill' by the boy soldier.
'Where is your father?'
Kill' by him too.

The men soldier force us all
Out of our place,
Say to the boy soldier –
Shoot us all dead.

All dead e'cept me.
My mother and father.
My brothers and sisters.
My grandmother.

Then the men soldier
Tell the boy soldier,
Marry me on the groun'.
They laughin'.

Then all the men
They force on me and beat me.
One of them cut off my hand
With a machete.

The boy soldier given so much drug
By the men soldier
He don't know anythin'.
He look sick. Very sick.

He look younger 'n me.
I thirteen years ol' today.
Baby growin' inside me
But I want to die.

And the boy soldier,
I want him to die.

A Few Comedies

Dramatis Personæ

Daverick, An Innkeeper
Holly, Molly & Polly, His Daughters
Gilbert, A Squire
Hector, The Squire's Son
Gwynedd, The Squire's Daughter
Ruddock, A Farmer
Thomas Akin, An Idiot Labourer
A Pilgrim

Act I, Scene I. Inside the Inn

   [Knocking at the door]

Rudd.: *(off-stage)* Open up!

From Whom

From whom one learns, one teaches.
From whom one teaches, one learns.
Molly-dolly clip-clop,
Bim-bam battle-axe.

The Four Truths

This story begins with a Young Person deciding to become a Seeker – to be devoted exclusively to seeking Truth.

After continuous journeying and enduring many hardships in the search, eventually a Teacher accepted this Seeker as a Student.

The Teacher said,

" My teaching is of The Four Truths. When I have finished speaking, you will pass the next year and a day in silent meditation, then return to me to complete the teaching.

The First Truth is that All Human Knowledge is contained within four areas:

>The Wisdom of The Soul,
>The Instinct of The Body,
>The Love of The Heart, and
>The Learning of The Mind.

The Second Truth is that although each area is distinctive at its core, its boundaries are defined only by the individual human being; the nature of

I. The Instinct of The Body

these boundary definitions is not inherent to the areas themselves, thus overlapping is a natural occurrence.

The Third Truth is that the area of The Wisdom of The Soul contains the other three areas and that from a point of view within this area there are no boundaries between the other areas: in fact the other areas do not exist, other than as concepts.

And finally, The Fourth Truth: there exists the area Outside All Human Knowledge, in which The Four Truths may not be true, and not only does the concept of finality have no relevant meaning or application, but the very concept of concepts themselves is non-existent.

My speaking will shortly end. In certain circumstances, an end comes as a blessed relief. I approach the conclusion of this teaching by saying that it may be understood that Ending cannot exist without Beginning: that there is neither ending nor beginning but rather end-begin-end and begin-end-begin. From which the question may arise,

'What is it that ends, is that what it begins?' "

The student was awestruck by this teaching and passed the following year and a day meditating upon it, thereafter returning to the teacher. Whatever was subsequently learned either could not be written or will never be written. Or perhaps was written and is now considered lost.

Whichever was the case, it's probably worth considering it to be entirely irrelevant to you and completely forgetting all about it, if you can.

The End

Self Taught

You wanna be taught to learn,
But you're too uptight!

You gotta learn to loosen up,
You gotta loosen up to learn.

A Seed In The Soil Explodes Slowly

You may be a woman
whereas I have no face
and may be dead

(we both know you're alive)

but let us go on together.

Finding Yourself

Person Y: I'm trying to find my true self,
              can you help me?

Person X: Get lost!

I Was Still Enough To Notice Anyway

I had one soft shoe on,
Then the carpet was all right,
But walking to the music
Seemed to take me all night,

And by the end
It was all tacky and sweet,
A sick old smell of rubber
Wisped the floor like a redcoat retreat.

I was defeated,
Lay back on the bed,
But the left shoe was twitching,
Like it knew something was coming.

Instead of being afraid
The carpet edge bit my toe
And I took fright like a blow on the head,
Then the light bulb blew in from all directions.

My big toe creaked in its damp sock.
Maybe it was in sympathy,
If it was then that's okay,
I was still enough to notice anyway.

(to Don)

Letter to Mr S. Irwin 17th June 1990

Now this is it: the carpet, the colours, the echo and the proximity, all together making a single event out of the flickering light between my foot and the warp and woof that sped through the fingers of other beings.

Hesitating to embrace their stylised reed-beds, my hesitation is instantaneously transformed into a psychic barrier of contracting guilt, which I have to shed in the manner of an insect shedding a skin; subsequently able to bask in the emanations of a Higher Intelligence.

Approaching a threshold of intimacy, tolerance questions rising up, I offer you these three gentle reminders:

    1. To re-experience conception is fatal
    2. The State emphasises gymnastics
    3. Versprung szczęśliwy Ockeghem.

Interview with General Stoppe

I'm talking today to General Stoppe. General, do you have any reason to suppose that –

No, I don't.

I'm sorry, I hadn't finished my question.

I finished it for you. It's finished, you're finished.

Well, let me put it to you in a different way then –

Absolutely not! In the negative imperative!

I beg your pardon, I was merely –

Beg? Beg? Get down on your knees! Outstretch your open palms! Wail and whine and plead as if your very life depended upon it!

Well, I'm not sure that is strictly necessary –

Then what are you sure is strictly necessary?

General, the word on the street is –

Stop! What? Stop looking, stop walking? Stop breathing, stop talking, stop thinking, stop up your ears, stop whatever you're doing? It is in fact quite specific: stop your forward motion. For your own safety and for the safety of others, as death or serious injury may otherwise result, you must come to a full stop. Not a half stop, or an empty stop, or any fraction of a stop. Stop is stop, no forward motion. Then one assesses the situation and determines when, how, and in which direction to begin moving forward again.

General, are you aware, you surely are, of –

Yes, I am.

What?

Yes, I am aware of it.

But I haven't said what it is yet.

You don't need to, I am already aware of it, as I have already said. There is no need to mention it again.

But I don't know what you're referring to.

I think you do.

Well, let me ask you then, are you referring to –

Yes.

Are you referring to the widely expressed criticism of your leadership, your flagrant disregard for basic human rights, for the rule of law and for common decency? To accusations of intimidation, nepotism and embezzlement? To allegations of dereliction of duty, abuse of power and sexual misconduct?

No, I was not referring to that.

Well, frankly, I am! What do you say to –

Forgive me but I say to you now what I have always said to peddlers of any such nonsense whenever I have come across it, whenever I have had the misfortune to come across it in my path, because there will always be the knockers, the petty cynics and critics, the mud-splashers and nit-pickers, the stirrers and so-called satirists, and the downright no-goods of course, and I always say to them what I now say to you, something that has stood me in jolly good stead whenever I have found myself in a sticky situation, it has become something of a motto for me really, no doubt you have heard it in my context before: Go bake a cake. And I am not just saying it, I mean it. Please go and do it now, or as soon as you can, as soon as you next go into your kitchen, because I absolutely guarantee your mood will improve as a consequence! At any rate, mine always does. Good-day to you!

Letter to the Editor of The T—

11th November 1983

Dear Sir,

I am hoping all television news broadcasts will now be included in the 'video nasty' category, consequently be banned, and the rapid decline of this 'Age of Information' thus initiated.

How can we allow anyone to be so arrogant as to assume responsibility for the lives of others, in the face of such an overload of information from the outside world, until such people have perceived and understood profoundly the internal messages coming continually from their own brains and bodies?

Yours sincerely etc

The T— November 17, 1983

PRIVATE

Dear Mr W—,

The Editor thanks you for the letter you kindly sent recently, which has been read with interest.

He regrets, however, it has not been possible to find a place for it in the correspondence columns.

Yours sincerely,

A Discursive Philosophy

I remember some things and forget others. Of all the things I've forgotten, I wonder what it would have been worth remembering. I know I'm reading some words in a book – could they really be blick and wit?

The greatest book of all could have only one word, if that one word were the highest quality word of all: the unknown name of God. Or would a book with no words whatsoever be of even higher quality, *reductio ad absurdum*? Very popular books have been written (for children) with perhaps no more than a hundred words. What is a book, after all? Perhaps a high-quality word, for example, 'mañana', repeated without punctuation 300 times on every page for 154 pages, would constitute a book of greater quality than one of 218 blank pages. Or is it all a matter of context – bookshop or stationery shop?

The Mañana book would probably appeal more to some readers with the insertion of one un-numbered blank page between pages 98 and 100, although seeing as no-one can read a blank page, perhaps 'book-owners' would be more accurate than 'readers'. In fact, there can be no perhaps about it – a book is judged by its reader. (In later chapters we will open an inquiry into the merits and effects of a consensus of opinion.) A book is perhaps no more or less an inanimate object than a framed painting or a digital recording of music; perhaps no more or less hungry for experiences of foreign cultures than an empty bucket. Perhaps 'perhaps' itself has no meaning. Peut-être on parle français mais toutes sont les mêmes choses. Hands measure horses, fingers spirits, and armies crawl on their bellies. (My eyes want to close whereas I want to read on.)

Why would anyone have a relationship with a book? This is an adrenaline question, raising the bio-chemical paradox, and the existence of any paradox proves, by the simplest process of elimination, the existence of a higher level of understanding, from which vantage point the paradox no longer carries its paradoxical characteristics – thus actually ceases to exist. Everything is beautiful once the beholder knows the nature of beholding.

Every question therefore has an answer merely by coming into being, all depends on the questioner/answerer's level of consciousness. So, we must take a leap of faith and consider the nature of that level of consciousness which transcends all scales of measurement.

At this 'level' (clearly we are now beyond all talk of levels), the animate and inanimate do not have any meaningful distinction and it is entirely possible to have a deep and meaningful relationship with a book since matter, light, and personality quirks are all one, and the fridge is eaten by the cucumber sandwich.

We now turn to reflect on the nature of reflection in general, and on this present reflecting in particular. To begin with, permit me to refer to the reference I made at the beginning of this sentence, to beginnings. It should be clear by now, to all but the meanest of intellects, that the concept of beginnings is no more than a mental construct. There is no actual beginning, of any shape or form, in reality.

Where does the river begin – at the spring, in the raincloud? Where does your own life begin – with your father's sperm, in the unfathomable voids of outer space? Where does a centimetre begin – at the third or fourth electron from the left? Where does this book, or your mind, begin; when did your relationship with it begin?

Questions that probe the limits of the mind itself. And at which the mind naturally complains.

The mind does not like to have its limitations paraded in front of you, or in front of itself; nor does it know for certain which of the two is worse.

'Never mind,' maybe your admirable response, because you believe that your mind, despite such stretches and probings, entertainments and challenges, will continue to exist. Therefore, in the spirit of bold explorers, we must consider existence without any presence of mind.

Is the mind capable of conceiving of an existence without itself? No.

Does such an existence exist? Yes.

But we find ourselves patrolling the edge of reason, and longing to cross into the realm where No and Yes are no longer necessary, in fact to where they don't exist at all (except as defining characteristics of a lower level of existence).

So we see with eyes open and shut, both.

'I see,' you say. You say I see.

'I see you,' I say. We see all of you, you see.

Let us now consider this book, or your mind, as a kind of computer connected to millions of other similar computers, with a human being operating each one.

A human, communicating with another human via, say, microchip, book, landline or electromagnetic wave, desires engagement in a relationship with the other human, not with the inanimate objects. We will return to the animate brain and telepathy in later chapters.

The point emerges at last (and in the bright sunlight of day seems blindingly obvious) that the human relationship is unique and cannot be replicated by anything non-human. Thus, a relationship with a book is not equivalent to a relationship with another person, it is a pale imitation, a ghost. Dare one say, a substitute.

If one speaks of having a relationship with a book, we assume (I'm assuming here that all such assumptions are examined by the reader in their own time) it is not the paper and ink that is being referred to, but rather the characters of the story, or, God help us, the author/reader; representations of people; ceci n'est pas une femme; approximations, dis-embodiments, of humans.

Where is the hammer of the gods?

Where are the rules of grammatical correctness or stylistic congruity being violated? Are they being broken through ignorance, or design? If ignorance, is this contemptible or forgivable? If design, is this successful or failuretic? After all, no wind has ever truly filled any sails.

Winch up the anchor, the Captain may say.

And what do you do?

You reply,

'I am not on board your vessel, Sir, I inhabit a different plane of existence. To me, you are no more than a feature of my imagination, albeit one assisted into being with the help of this book I'm reading, which is where you first appeared. I can tell you that your anchor has turned into a bucket of strawberry ice-cream which your crew are now fighting over in a frenzy of greed so passionate that they do not even hear your commands.

You now take off all your clothes and dive into the sea. Ha! Captain indeed! Now we see who the real Captain is. Don't look at me like that. Swim to that island. The native girls will treat you like a king.'

And here the closing quotation mark indicates that your response to the Captain has come to a close. Will you say anything more to the former Captain? Will we hear any more of his adventures, past, present or future?

The first-time reader can only guess. The author, as he or she writes, may not know either, at this stage.

But at this stage the author does know because now the book is finished so of course the author knows everything, and I believe everything I read.

For example, a Sardine tin is not a Hessian sack.

Letter To The Editor   24th March 2007

Sir,

    I love it, when I am driving in my car with the radio on, that the very first bulletin of traffic news I hear never fails to remind me that what I have been, and am, listening to is in fact exceedingly irritating, and then I come to my senses and turn the radio off.

    I would be delighted, by your publishing of this letter, to highly recommend this course of action to all your readers. And, may I add, other applications of the same principle can easily be found, eg. in the substitution of 'reading' for 'listening'; 'letters page' for 'bulletin of traffic news'; 'newspaper' for 'radio', and 'chuck in the recycling bin' for 'turn off'.

    I have never been, Sir, nor ever will be, your servant, obedient or otherwise, —

Chaque Jour   (to J-P S.)

Chaque jour les journaux des imbéciles,
Chaque jour mes amis embrassent la mort.
Le monde est toujours la même chose,
Óu est ma joie de vivre?

A Provocative Cellist

A cellist provoked a great scandal
By refusing to play any Handel
Unless he could wear
His right foot quite bare
And his left in an open-toed sandal.

Concert Review
by Our Music Critic

The programme was devoted to two world premieres for solo piano, *I Can, So I Will* and *Make A Mess Of It*, both performed by the composer Osman Rubyat. The prominent feature of the first piece was a series of interspersed interruptions, in which the pianist rose to his feet and announced with a dignified bow, 'Good evening, lentils and jaded men'.

Having begun playing in traditional fashion with his fingers on the keys, Rubyat resumed after each of these pauses with a new implement. We were treated to demonstrations of his skill, not only on the keys but over the entire constituent parts of the piano, with: a violin bow, a pearl necklace, a hammer, a stick of celery and a silk scarf. After no more than a few minutes I had the distinct impression that Mr Rubyat's show was repellent, demonstrating neither substance nor depth.

It was, however, during *Make A Mess Of It* that a unique and shocking scandal unfolded in dramatic fashion. Having draped both scarf and necklace around his neck, jammed the violin bow into the open strings and eaten the celery, Rubyat took the lump hammer in his hand and astonishingly began smashing up the piano, a Steinway grand worth around £60,000, with pointedly rhythmic blows.

For the first time I, and everyone present, sat up and took notice. Not only was it an unforgettable sound, but the frisson of outrage that swept through the auditorium was unlike anything I have ever experienced in a concert hall.

With the management clearly in shock and Mr Rubyat refusing all initial attempts to persuade him to bring his performance to a close, a team of security personnel had no choice but to forcibly restrain him, providing a quite remarkable spectacle that will live long in the memory, whereas Mr Rubyat's career, as a pianist at least, is surely at an irretrievable end and sources inside the venue are hinting that he is likely to be charged with criminal damage.

I earnestly hope he gets his day in court, and if he does that I can be there to witness it. A dreadful, historic evening.

Come Again?

A hushed sports hall, the floor-space filled with formal rows of identical desks, students taking a written examination. The Invigilator is seated at his table on a rostrum at the far end. As the big clock's minute hand touches 12, he stands up and announces,

'And now, Paper Two!'

A bikini-clad young beauty enters smiling from a door in the corner, carrying a large gold envelope, which she hands to the Invigilator.

'Thank you, Krystal.'

Krystal turns to the students, strikes a pose and recites her line,

'As you know, only those who pass Paper One can go on to Paper Two!'

Pouts and exits. Invigilator opens the gold envelope.

'And here it is ... now let's see what we have here ... Question Forty-Two: Where does the status quo end and insanity begin?'

A nun bursts in from the same door; we see it is Krystal in a nun's costume. She hurries to her place, clearly marked by two short strips of grey tape stuck in the shape of a cross on the floor, and melodramatically exclaims,

'The city is flooded and we are entirely cut off!'

A bearded young man in a cream linen jacket then sidles in, walks past her into the hall holding both arms wide open and declares,

'Hello everyone, it's me, Jesus! I'm back!'

Some Songs Without Their Notes

Coulda Been A Buddha

Coulda been a Buddha
But I met a pretty girl,
Contemplatin' meditatin'
But I wanna see the world.

Coulda been a Buddha
But I got me a guitar,
Coulda been a Buddha
But for Psycho Delia.

Coulda been a Buddha
But baby, can't you see?
Though I coulda been a Buddha
I'd rather just be me.

A Song For Julian's 50th Birthday

*(transcript of an introduction to a live recording,
Harberton Village Hall, April 2003)*

Good evening.
[READS] Crowd go wild with excitement.
(Applause, cheers & whistles from the audience.)
Thank you. I'd like to take just a minute now to introduce my band,
[TURNS TO SEE ONLY ONE MUSICIAN]
on bass, drums, lead guitar, backing vocals and piano: Mr Nicky M— !! We've just flown all the way round the world to be with you here tonight, Nicky's got a return ticket . . .
But seriously now, Julian, A— , G— , S— , distinguished visitors, ladies and gentlemen, friends, kids, cats, babies born and unborn, you're probably all sitting there thinking: he's about to sing a song!
Well, you could not be more wrong.
No.
Because this song is in fact a duet.
That's right.
And now it is my great privilege to introduce to you, my singing partner for this evening, move over Robbie, because yes, all the way from Los Angeles, star of stage and screen, ladies and gentlemen, may I present:
MISS – NICOLE – KIDMAN!!
(Nobody enters.)
(Audience gradually accepting the reality.)
[WITH FINGER IN EAR] Uh-uh, yes?
Oh, really? That's a real shame, yeah!

Okay, thanks.

[LOOKS AT FINGER] Wow, one more thing for a finger to do.

Well, word has just reached me that Miss Kidman is on a Cruise in the Mediterranean.

Julian, I'm sorry, I really am.

Okay, on with the show.

Now, those of you with a rounded musical education will know at least some of the works of the 20th-century American composer Frank Zappa. Anybody here not familiar with that great man's contribution, go check him out! I'm going to attempt something now that Uncle Frank used to love! Most people know this particular activity, *that we are going to try right here this evening,* as 'audience participation'. Frank used to call it 'enforced recreation'. In other words, do you have a choice?

No.

But don't worry, it's very easy, it's a lot of fun, and here's how it works: at the end of every verse I have the line:

'And the crowd cries out – '

and you all respond: 'Julian's the man!'

Let's try that. *(Rehearsal of the audience.)*

Then there's the second line, where I sing:

'And Julian replies',

and then Julian, you sing: 'Here I am!'

Let's try that. *(Rehearsal of Julian.)*

Right then, we're all ready.
Now, there are two things of interest in this song, first is that there is a composer mentioned by name and I want to be specific about the name so there's no misunderstanding, the composer's name is
Rick Man-Enough.
The second much more important thing is that I want to apologise in advance to A—, for the first verse in particular, because there is a reference to some minor film actress or other and, well, you can probably guess the rest.
And if you can't, don't worry, because here it comes now.
Okay Nicky, let's do the song!
(Not too fast now . . .)

> Nicole comes out the Oscars
> and she's feeling pretty low,
> No shiny little man to hold,
> no mantelpiece-y glow,
> No Tom, no Dick, no Harry,
> in fact she's home alone,
> Now who would like to ring her bell
> and make her sweat 'n moan?
>
> > And the crowd cries out, *"Julian's the man!"*
> > And Julian replies, *"Here I am!"*
>
> We take you now into the woods,
> a quite enchanting view,
> Where Snow White's traipsing through the trees
> but without her motley crew;

For she's frustrated, yes, she's bored,
and quite gone off her food!
" Oh, for grown-up pleasures,
and to hear some jokes – quite rude! "

   And the crowd cries out, *etc.*

A composer called Rick Man-Enough
has penned a masterpiece,
Eleven notes in every chord,
will wonders never cease!
" I need a performer! " the maestro exclaims,
" For the premiere in November!
Someone with ten fingers true
and a dextrous male member! "

   And the crowd cries out, *etc.*

Steely Dan are on the road
and having quite a ball,
They roll on into Totnes,
gonna rock the Civic Hall!
The lights go down, the band walks on,
but one of them falls off the stage!
What they need now is a cool jazzman –
Of a certain age!

   And the crowd cries out, *etc.*

A Dumb Song

I want to write a dumb song,
A dumb song with long words in it,
But I just can't think of one.
Back off! Just give me some time here!
I will find those long words
And then put them in this song.
I want to write a dumb song,
A dumb song with long words.

I am a young man, from the US of A,
And I live with my Mom and Dad,
And they think I am dumb
And all the songs I sing are too,
But I'll show them!
I'll write a dumb song with long words in,
That will show them
That I am dumb by free choice,
Not 'cos I am dumb.
It makes me mad when Dad tells me I'm dumb!
Now all I need is some words
Of more than one syllable –

Good! I've done it!
But that's not the end,
Now I'll develop this linguistic theme!
Because dumb is not stupid,
Dumb is being unable to speak.
Which is different.
What's stupid about that?
Nothing!

Come on America,
Wake up and speak your mind!

I'm not mad, I'm angry!
Which is different.
Mad is more like insane,
I'm not insane when I'm angry!
Don't call me dumb, let me have my voice!
Don't call me mad, let me have my rage!
And I let you have yours,
Or are we not human?

Come on America!
Wake up and hear what you're really saying!

Come on everybody,
What do you tell yourself?
There is – come on, listen carefully now,
Maybe, just maybe,
There is something you want to change
In the language and attitude
You've settled on for yourself.

I know, I'm not much of a role model,
All I wanted was to write a dumb song
With long words in it,
But at least I have achievalised that.

That's a start.

Acoustic/Electric Christmas Song

(acoustic)

This is such a lovely song,
And it isn't very long!
I think we can all agree
It is nice and Christmassy
And you can all love me!

(electric crunch squeak beep feedback fuzz)

Words don't rhyme in the songs I write
And I can't even tune my guitar up!

I hate all of you fat lazy bastards,
And you can all hate me!
That's the only thing we can be sure of
In this hell-world –
Hate, hate, hate, hate!

Yeah!

Garden Gnome Choices

Why don't you go
Back to your garden gnomes?
Don't you feel sorry for the little hard men,
Sitting by the pond all day?
Hands on their rods
But they never catch nods,
And you can see there's fish in the pond,
In the shade of the willow frond.

You could make them simulate sex,
Or smash them into a million specks.
Then you could spend your life
Gluing them back together with a knife.
What an achievement that would be!
All your friends would come and see,
When you'd finished,
Aged one-hundred-and-three.

You could spend your days
Dreaming in a purple haze.

You could spend your nights
In imaginary nylon tights,

Re-designing kites.

I Always Know What You're Thinking

Don't look, because you might have
an unattractive surprise.
I know what you're looking at,
it's that scene before your very eyes.

Don't breathe, because the air's not fresh,
some days that's how it goes.
I know what you're smelling,
it's that smell right under your nose.

Don't strain your little ear drums
just to pick out the background hiss.
I know what you're hearing,
it's a sound that sounds like this.

Don't imagine yourself dying
or being born again.
I know what you're thinking,
it's that thought passing through your brain.

Don't fake those fine emotions,
who's fooled by what they feel / do?
I know who you're in love with,
it's someone quite a bit like me / you.

Don't scream, it's just a bad dream.
Why say you will, knowing you won't?
I know how you're feeling,
you feel good and then you don't.

Don't eat up all those cultures,
you're so far-fetched, they're just far-flung.
I know what you taste like,
just like me but with your own tongue.

Don't talk unless you want to,
I've heard your voice and you've heard mine.
I know what you've been saying,
stringing words along a spoken / broken line.

O Chooser!

we are in a suicidal state
on this spinning globe in space
we are all choosers
don't you be abusers
collective unconsciousness
we are all one in the light of the One Source

life
tree from a seed
love from a smile
living with truth
ridding myself of self-delusion
filling myself with a loving-living fusion
life after decision
to be or not to be
profound simplicity

O chooser!
what do you have in mind
that cannot be defined?
nuclear weaponry
suicidal capability
you have response-ability?

life
collective unconsciousness
like a flower to the rising sun
you are
to the dawn of enlightenment

It Was Very Good

Trees, grow tall!
Grass, grow small!
Babies, crawl!
Night, fall!
Morning, break!
Mountains, quake!
Sleepers, wake!
Hands, shake!
Lovers, sigh!
Towels, dry!
Saucers, fly!
Shoppers, buy!
Dancers, reel!
Fingers, feel!
Curates, kneel!
Wounded, heal!
Sinners, sin!
Losers, win!
Ends, begin!
Spiders, spin!
Flames, flare!
Glasses, stare!
Mothers, care!
Angels, dare!

Workers, toil!
Wires, coil!
Kettles, boil!
Spoilers, spoil!
Bombs, explode!
Guns, reload!
Codes, decode!
Steel, corrode!
Firewood, spit!
Atoms, split!
Judges, sit!
Gloves, fit!
Flowers, sleep!
Carpets, creep!
Candles, leap!
Dishes, bleep!
Lava, slow!
Rivers, glow!
You think you know
you think
Stop

but do you?

Nothin' Blues

got no money
got no food
got no job
got no roof

got no shirt
got no shoes
got no bed
ain't even got the blues

Aiee!
got the
I-gotta-whole-lotta-nothin',
Nothin' Blues!

got no body
got no soul
got no rock
got no role

got no holds
got no news
got no goals
ain't even got the blues

Aiee!
got the
I-gotta-whole-lotta-nothin',
Nothin' Blues!

Gospel Song

[Chorus]

Let's make time, let's make love,
Let's be friends, with God above.
Enough of hate, enough of fear,
Only love is real here.

We all know the time will come,
We will ride into the setting sun.
Let's not wait till that final day
To open our hearts and hear what God has to say:

[Chorus]

Hear what I'm singing now in my song,
When you feel it, sing along.
It's just a reminder, you might well say,
That we all need loving every night and day.

[Chorus]

More Innocence & Experience

Messages From God

On receiving a message from God,
(Though his wife did regard it as odd)
The vicar would say,
' I have to obey! '
And he did buy a new fishing rod.

At breakfast he once said, ' Oh dear!
I'm suddenly called on to smear
Some butter and jam,
Thin slices of ham
And honey all over your rear! '

Strawberries And Champagne

We could go skiing – the mountains of France,
Let's go to Cuba and learn how to dance.
We can go anywhere, and nowhere's mundane,
When you bring the strawberries,
And I bring the champagne!

[Chorus]

> *If you're the rose, then I'll be the bee,*
> *If you're the salt, then I'll be the sea,*
> *If you're the lock, then I'll be the key,*
> *And you can be you, and I can be me.*

We could watch Paris from the Eiffel Tower,
Let's just canoodle in the park for an hour.
We could hop onto the overnight train –
You bring the strawberries, I'll bring the champagne.

We could go touring, right down to Rome,
Or then again, darling, just stay at home!
But when we go cruising on the Mediterrane' –
You bring the strawberries, I'll bring the champagne.

We could canoe up the Tay from Dundee,
Let's watch the whales in the Icelandic Sea!
Whatever we do, darling, one thing is plain –
We have to have strawberries!
Strawberries and champagne!

Under The Sea

As I was walking
Under the sea,
I met a little shellfish
Who looked like me.

I said, 'Hello there!
What's your name?'
Sorrowfully, it said to me,
'Do you think life's a game?'

There Was A Big Fish In The Sea

There was big fish in the sea
Who said, 'Little fish, come and see!
My dining-room suite
Is now all complete
And you're all invited to tea!'

But one little fish called out, 'Wait!
My grandmother used to relate
Long tales of woe
About those who go
To tea and end up on his plate!'

A Student Of Goethe

A student of Goethe declared,
'My freedom will not be impaired,
I may not be able
To dance on this table
But I would if I knew that you cared!'

Jack Shepherd

There once was a shepherd called Jack
Who had a remarkable knack
For herding his sheep
While he was asleep,
And dreaming that he was a yak.

Literary Alien

Once, along a long country road,
I lost my way because it really snowed.
And then I saw an alien,
Reading *Pygmalion*,
Look up at me with eyes that glowed.

The Wishful-Thinking Jungle Song

Down among the jungle plants
There's lots of funny things to watch
And eat.

You can sit up in a tree and laugh
And listen to the jungle sounds,
Perhaps pretend you are a monkey.

There are animals of all shapes and sizes
All over the place,
Everywhere you look!

The jungle is in fact rather crowded in my opinion.

Hungry Choices

A hungry youth happened to find
A length of half-chewed bacon rind.
He said, 'If I knew
Who'd done the half-chew
Then I'd know which way I was inclined!'

No Nursery Rhyme

I don't want to!
I don't want to!
Oink oink, woof woof,
All fall down!

I'm not playing!
I'm not playing!
Baa baa, mew mew,
All fall down!

I don't like you!
I don't like you!
Go away! I want to
Play by myself!

I want Mummy!
I want Mummy!
You're not nice at all,
I want to go home!

Observed

A monk who'd meditated through the night,
Observed the rising sun, which was so bright
He had to look away,
And then was heard to say,
'In truth, this morning, I have seen the light!'

Both Good

I once took a walk in a wood
To think about whether I should
Go climb up a tree
Or go home for tea –
In the end I did both, which was good!

In My Spa   (to Abel)

It's true, have a look, there they are!
VIPs of all kinds in my spa!
A King, a tycoon,
A Prince from Rangoon,
A Bishop, a Queen and a Tsar!

The Uneducated Baroness

The uneducated Baroness of Slough
Tried to give an explanation as to how
The sound of a word
Can be seen and not heard –
But she couldn't, the ignorant cough!

Lots Of Tea

A woman who lived by the coast
Fell madly in love with a post.
Whilst talking of nails
And woodlice and snails,
They drank lots of tea and ate toast.

A Moral Tale Of Reading While Eating

A hairy subscriber to Punch
Was reading while eating his lunch,
He saw a cartoon
About a baboon
And came to a relative crunch.

A Career In Politics

In Cabinet meetings Brezhnev
Would often pretend to be deaf,
And it is my belief
He'd have had much relief
If he'd gone back to being a chef.

Santa Claus Defiant

There once was a Santa named Claus
Who used to see chimneys as doors,
But how his big bot
Got through the pot
Defies all the physical laws!

Shout, Hooray!

It gives me great pleasure to say,
It's been a most wonderful day,
With good food and wine,
And sport very fine,
So let us now all shout, 'Hooray!'

Proud

There once was a woman of Stroud
Who of her bra size was most proud.
She'd toss back her hair
And invite us to stare
At what made her stand out from the crowd.

The Duke Who Went Too Far

There once was a noble – a Duke –
Who loved to talk gobbledegook.
But he once went too far
With his dearest Mama
And earned a quite shocking rebuke.

On The Virtue Of Being Polite

An interesting slant on the virtue
Of being polite: it won't hurt you.
Give thanks for a gift,
Give nonsense short shrift,
Then no-one can ever pervert you.

What Gavin Ate

It was green,
it was gluey,
it smelled like wet dog,
it was a bit like a fried egg
and it looked dead.

Alice poked it with a stick,
Mary didn't like it,
Gavin picked it up
and quietly swallowed it
while the girls shrieked
and soon afterwards he was sick.

Later, he was building a sandcastle,
yelled at Alice
when she accidentally trod in it.

Now he's trying to get his big toe
into his mouth.

My Lanky Donkey

I had a lanky donkey
His legs were never short.
He liked to gambol with the lambs,
Or so I'd always thought.

Although he was so wilful –
Gave me quite the run-around!
It's good to let them do their thing,
Or so I thought I'd found.

But he had to run round backwards!
Attempt a mid-air somersault!
And then he blamed me for his injuries!
But of course they weren't my fault!

I left him at a sanctuary
Where he looked me in the eye,
He didn't speak but I heard him say,
'I'm gonna learn to fly.'

I haven't seen him since that day
But a rumour reached my ear
That he'd gone abroad and changed his name
From Bert to Vladimir.

O, Most Beautiful Gnat!

This happened when I was
On the dark side of the Earth.

I was inside a room,
Sitting up in bed,
Darkness all around the edge
Of the lamplight

Which was shining on the book
That I was holding and reading –

On the bright page abruptly appeared the finest
Gnat,
Wings green, body black,
Feathery radar antennae vibrating.

'O, most beautiful Gnat,
I know you know,
Please tell me where it's at!'

Foul Habits

A fellow with habits most foul,
Whose face wore a permanent scowl,
On black slugs he'd feast,
A hundred at least,
And at passers-by he would howl.

Riddled And Diddled (to Olly)

Riddled and diddled
And piddled and popped,
Now I have started,
Now I have stopped.

Dark like a starling,
Soft like a kiss,
Nothing can
Ever again
Be like this.

No Rhyme

There once was a word with no rhyme,
Now lost in the grey mists of thyme,
There wasn't one poem
That that word would go in —
Now ain't that a bleedin' great shyme?

I Loved My Car

High-powered woman executive leaves futuristic office building, gets into back seat of waiting limousine.

'I want to go to Paris, James.'

'Understood,' the car's computer replies.

The engine starts and the car pulls away, driving itself. The computer says,

'Would you like a bath?'

'Oh James, that would be marvellous!'

Part of the seat converts automatically into a bath. Woman executive undresses and slides into the steamy water. Car says,

'A new device was fitted today.'

The woman moans for some time with mounting pleasure.

Cut to an interior, a hybrid bedroom-garage. Lying on a large bed, woman executive gives birth to two shiny identical little cars, one blue, one pink. Where she might have had breasts, the woman executive has two miniature fuel pumps. The midwife, in overalls, guides the little cars to the pumps and fills them up. The midwife, inspecting the cars, says,

'Both sets of four wheels are all fine, headlights not working yet but that's quite normal. Keep them clean, a good wash inside and out every Sunday morning is usually sufficient, it's important to change their oil regularly, and keep your eye on the tyre pressures. Aren't they lovely!'

'Tis The Season

How did good Saint Nicholas
Become this Santa Claus?
It's a story of our time
That gives us cause to pause:

For to advertise some fizzy pop
In the good ol' USA,
That's how the red fat fellow was born,
So those in the know do say.

But 'tis the season to ease off strife
And see how new love starts,
To find ourselves with faith in life
And feel goodwill in all our hearts.

Frigid Maureen

A pianist born in Armagh,
Was regarded world-wide as a star,
With rousing sea-shanties
Written out on her panties,
And Boulez all over her bra.

Her house on the island of Nairn
Could not be described as moderne.
Her name was Maureen,
She smelled of chlorine,
And so did Roberta her bairn.

Regarding her breasts, which were rounded,
I looked on with passion unbounded.
My member was rigid
But Maureen was frigid
So I was completely confounded.

Sorrowful Peter's Tale

A sorrowful fellow named Peter
Was knocking back wine by the litre.
He said, 'I'll explain
Why I'm going insane –
All because of a dark señorita!'

'We met in down-town Barcelona,
She had an amazing persona,
I thought it was love
But she gave me the shove
And I wish now that I'd never known her!'

A Lover In Fife

An eminent fellow of Yale,
One morning perusing his mail,
Was heard to cry out –
To actually shout –
And then to collapse with a wail!

The man was found having a cry,
And was asked, 'My good fellow, why?'
– 'Because try as I might
I can't make it right!'
Came back his pathetic reply.

'Now look here,' continued his friend,
'You sound like the world's going to end!
Your sobbing and moaning,
Your weeping and groaning,
Are driving me right round the bend!'

The fellow said, 'Look at this letter!
Really, I should have known better!
It's addressed to my wife
From her lover in Fife!'
And he cried till his socks were much wetter.

No Puck

There was a young lady of Gaul
Who adored any game with a ball,
But mention a puck
And she'd answer, 'Tough luck!
I don't fancy that sort at all!'

Nice Can't Always Be Nice

Well, Nice can't always be nice;
Cannes can be a den of vice!
And Cagnes-sur-mer?
We don't go there.

A Holiday Romance

Te quiero, Pizza Maria,
Mia bolsa del amorosa,
Hasta luego sangria,
¡Contigo tapas con carne!

Uno, cuatro, ocho tortillas,
Algo mas? De nada.
¡Que bolsa de las mantequillas,
Buenos días Esther Notchay!

Be Quiet

Moonlight on the hive,
Wax has sealed the honeycomb,
The bee is silent.

> *The author reckons it highly unlikely*
> *that this is an original joke,*
> *but at least here it is in an original form.*

A Conclusion

Considering all of the facts,
And all relevant Statutory Acts,
One has to conclude
That to shop in the nude
Requires one to be quite relaxed.

A Tardy Bus Driver

A tardy bus driver said, 'Sorry –
Me bus got attached to a lorry.
I sounded me 'orn,
But by then 'e 'ad gorn
And dropped us off down at the quarry!'

A Fellow's Cabinet

A Fellow of Classics at Oxford
Had a cabinet made out of boxwood.
Too small for his shoes
Or even his trews,
Though nothing else fitted his socks would.

A Bright Little Thing

Reciting, one evening, a verse
He'd composed in praise of his nurse,
A young man refrained
To mention he'd sprained
His ankle, and that it felt worse.

But the nurse was a bright little thing,
And noticed the state he was in.
With a bandage applied
And all the tears dried
She turned back the sheets and jumped in.

The Money Tree

Carefully plant a £20 note,
watering it in, etc.

In time, a tree grows.

It has flowers,
each petal is a brand new £20 note.

Pick a few,
take them indoors,
put them in a sandwich.
Eat it.

A Staunch Vegetarian Boy

A staunch vegetarian boy
One lunchtime was heard to shout, 'Oi!
This horrible meat
I will surely not eat,
I want everything made out of soy!'

His father said, 'Even your shoes?
To me this all sounds like bad news!
No eggs, fish or milk?
And what about silk?
Don't expect me to change, I refuse!'

His son replied, 'All meat is junk.
And I'm off to pack my old trunk.
Tomorrow I'll be
In a ship on the sea –
And live all my life as a monk!'

His mother said, 'Oh, what a day!
I only have one thing to say:
If you go and pack
Then I don't want you back – '
And the boy said, 'All right then, I'll stay!'

The Wolf-Man

Run, little lambs!
The Wolf-Man is coming!
No cooking-pot
But he wants his supper hot!

He wants to

Bite your neck,
Drink your blood,
Eat your flesh,
Suck your bones –

Make your body
Into his own!

Run, little lambs!
The Wolf-Man is coming!
No cooking-pot
But he wants his supper hot!

Aching Hearts

What Matters In This Relationship

What the hell did I see in you?
It's also here, in me,
To be seen.

What did I do,
Rejecting you for what's also here in me,
Waiting to be accepted?

What really matters in this relationship,
more than any content or form?

Only the nature of our commitments,
to ourselves,
to each other,
to our relationship.

Conscious or unconscious,
They exist.

And are having their effect.

My Love Balloon

One little prick, that's all it took,
To burst my love balloon.
My head can't make sense of this,
My heart feels torn in two,

For my woman's gone and left me
For another man,
Left me in pieces crying,
Fighting to understand

How one day it's, 'I love you',
And the next, she's in his bed!
Lord, have mercy on us,
I feel like I'm half dead.

*   *   *   *

These times now are hard times
That I'm living through,
Having to learn to love myself
More than I loved you.

Without Your Lights

Why are you
one of the ones
who drives along
without your lights on
in the dark,
through this darkest night?
like a gangster on the run,
on the slide,
your one last heist go wrong?
nothing to lose now,
nowhere to run to,
down on your luck,
no looking back,
a desperado?
like a housewife in a breakdown,
one too many evenings in,
just the two of you?
why did you buy the lie
of getting away from it all?
of believing you could hide
anything?
If you could only see yourself
now.

My Love Is Leaving

My love, I must leave you.
Just as no-one can deny
That the oceans are deep
And the mountains are high,

So the hour will come
When it's time for goodbye
And I will leave you, my darling one,
And you will leave me,

That's just the way it has to be.
And as we laugh and cry
Over all we've seen go by,
It's still you I want here by my side

To tell you that my love will never die
You are my love I kiss goodbye.

Do Not Read These Words

Love me, love me,
Do not heed me.

Do not say, 'I love you',
Do not touch my body.

Do not feed and clothe me,
Do not want or need me.

Do not make me happy.
Do not make me sane.

Do not read [hear] these words,
Love me, love me.

The Tall Young Man

Come home to find the tall young man,
child-minder for the evening,
smoking in the sitting-room.

So incensed I attack him,
I go mad with rage
and literally throw him out
through the front door.

He comes back later with his Mum
and she starts shouting at me,
on my doorstep.
Then a neighbour joins in.

The two of them light up.
I know it is only to provoke me
but I go crazy anyway, scare them yelling,
and push them away, back into the street.

They slope off up the hill, trailing threats.
I go back indoors
throw myself on the sofa,
so angry I'm weeping!

And then of course
both children quietly appear,
in their pyjamas,
and they're crying too.

Adrift

So you cut yourself off from me.

What good, then, can I possibly do
Except bid you 'adieu',
And wish you 'bon chance',
And hope you wash up on the beaches of France,
Where just to buy bread,
Say sorry,
Or hello,
You must speak in the language of love.

Willy-Willy Dong!

Oh Willy!
Willy-Willy Dong!

Willy-Willy Dong,
Dong ding-dong!

Oh Willy!
Willy-Willy Dong!

Willy-Willy,
Done no wrong!

I Am Free Now

I am not my clothes
I am not my face
I am not someone else
I am not this place

I am not what belongs to me
I am not yours or mine
I am not my skin
I am not this time

nor the voices of my mind
I am free now
I am
I am

ATOMBENOUGHTIMEANDERANGEL

My womb-tomb is warm on a winter morning,
I rise and live again in a cold, old world.
Could I be a demon with the power of the darkness,
Or am I resurrected as a servant of the Lord?

I Could Tell You Something
About Stravinsky

It's cold,
I'm outside, in the wrong clothes.
I'm going through it.

People look at me and are offended,
With their eyes they say to me,
" What! Are *you* still here?
Haven't they killed you yet? "
As if they didn't know who they are.

Death fear in their eyes,
Blind and lost in their eyes.
Or in me.
I'm going through it.

Then I'm inside a recording, playing back,
My brain is just a machine head.
Nothing but different shapes of sound.
But I don't speak.
I can't say, " I love you. "

Nobody judge!
The Judge of judges can crush you with nothing.

Draw no conclusions,
Make no assumptions,
We are alive together now,
Having the time of our lives.

I Want To Do Something Else

I wanted to do that
but now I'm doing this instead.

I want to do that
But I think when I'm doing that
I'll want to do this again.
Or something else.

But I think when I'm doing something else
I'll want to do something else.

I want to kill you.

One Of The Voices

There is a wonderful peace here

but one of the voices
whispers its way in
interested in anything
very soon it's talking
talking constantly
constantly getting louder
louder
SHOUTING INSANITIES

unless I notice
and stop it
then

There is a wonderful peace here

Ending

Deep Joy   (to Fred)

What a blessing,
after missing the boat,
after travels so remote,
to come home.

What a blessing,
when I'm dead on my feet,
to lie my body down,
rest and sleep,
and wake up with a sunrise!

What a blessing,
such deep joy,
when I meet my brother,
to be led by quiet waters.

As You Walk

You walk,

And as you walk, you wake,
And as you wake, a light shines out,

It shines in you,
It shines all around,
It shines on you,
It shines down,

It breathes you,
It feeds you,
It loves you,
It lives you,

It is you.

Writer's Block

The writer's head lowers down
Slowly groundwards,
Downwards, lowering gently nearer,
Drifting off to sleep,
Out of the window
With the birdsong
And the white clouds sliding,
Life is all outside,
Adrift on a raft
In a wide, open, flat, ocean desert,
A raft of old planks,
And ends of rope
Fraying and loosening
Whilst the sharks circle tighter,
The writer's head lowers,
Finally rests
On the block
And the axe chops.

A Prayer For Today's Truth-Seekers

(to Adrian)

My dear Earthly Mother,
With love
You gave me this body
And this world,
Made of infinite wonders.

My dear Divine Father,
With love
You gave me this spirit,
This breath of life –
I am one of Your breaths.

Mother, Father, I thank You for these gifts.
Anything more beautiful,
More miraculous, more exquisite,
I cannot imagine.

All I have, You have given me.

I dedicate my life,
Which is the flower of Your sacred union,
To You, my dear Mother,
To You, my dear Father.

For this body,
Which came from You
And is sustained by You,
Shall return to You.

For this spirit,
Which came from You
And is sustained by You,
Shall return to You,

That time will come.
But in this moment,
You are living in me.

May I so honour You
With every step,
With every breath.

We Are Here

Clearly,
Love what is.

Simply,
Let yourself be as you are
And change as you do.

This is all we are here for,
And we are here for all this,
For the whole of life.
I am here with you,
Love me.

My Goodbyes (God Be With You)

Goodbye to all my family and friends,
To laughter, good food, to music, and dancing,

Goodbye to all my dreams and plans,
To my home, my lover,
and to all my favourite places on this earth,

Goodbye to all my memories, to the moon and stars,
To warming sunshine, the sea,

Goodbye to everywhere I've never been,
To everyone I've never seen and now never will,

Goodbye to the entire space-time continuum
And all that it contains – farewell!

Hello to everything else!

Afterword

by Mwuetsi Ngwe Hakata

What age do you think you were when you learned to read?

Just for fun, assume the following is in fact true: there is much more for you to learn about what reading is – it doesn't need to be the same as last time, you can discover new ways that are more enlivening, more satisfying, more enjoyable than you ever knew or thought of before.

Here's a possibility:

Your eyes look over the paper and ink as usual, but now take yourself through the curtain of words and into your lucid and vivid imaginings. While you are reading, also be noticing more and more all your responses, including all your physical senses, giving yourself increasingly freer permission to feel and engage your entire emotional range.

Provide whatever amount of time you need to deeply drink everything in; smell, taste, touch and feel it, fully live it all. Feel free to speak aloud, shout, move about, sing and dance, feel the sensations and inspirations that life is transmitting through the writer, and that the writer is transmitting through the words, *directly to you.*

Enter this new relationship like a holy sacrifice, totally surrendered and wholehearted, openly allowing your emotional and physical being to join in more and more with your mental activity, restoring the balance and living the real dance of living.

This makes reading, and just about anything, a deeper, more alive and more fulfilling experience.

As with any new way, developing ways of practicing it that are the most enjoyable for you, the better your results.

Bon voyage, mes amis!

Artists

Clio Wondrausch . . . . *front cover*
Claudia Schmid Riley *85, 90, 93*
Moon Leith *15, 79, 111*
Lawrence Hassan *83, 99, 103*
Bram Stoker *35*
Wadiz *13, 131*
Martin Walker *87*

Clio Wondrausch

Ecstasea (cover picture) painted with found earth pigments. Thru the birthing cave she is dancing ecstatically with the vast, deep sea, dressed in seaweed and whirling a great frond of kelp.

To me, the Earth is Mother, giver of life. Her rich, warm colours are a raw and potent medium for expressing our creativity. Nature is always dancing and singing. My natural response is to dance and sing.

Exhibitions, prints, cards, originals, performance, courses...

37 Smithfields, Totnes, Devon, TQ9 5LR, UK.
+44 (0)1803 865836

www.wildhearth.co.uk

Claudia Schmid Riley

Claudia is an illustrator, Javanese dance teacher & performer, and is the designer of Dutzi soft-toys.

Previous publications:

> *In Wolle wickelt sich das Schaf*
> Peter Hammer 2003.
> ISBN 387 294 926 8

> *Schabernack*
> Peter Hammer 2002.
> ISBN 387 294 897 0
> Winner of the Troisdorf Award
> for picture-book illustration.

> *Bootdog*
> Aporia Press 1991.
> ISBN 948 518 91X

Commissions welcome for illustrations, picture stories & soft toys.

Email - claudia.dutzi@googlemail.com

Moon Leith

BA (Hons) Photography

I like cameras and tea and wagging my chin creatively with lovely, interesting people.

Email - leithmoonlily@googlemail.com

Lawrence Hassan

BA (Hons) Graphic Design

Technical assistance.

www.lawrencehassan.co.uk

Bram Stoker

BA (Hons) PGD Media Studies

Awards

1994 National Review of Live Art, Glasgow.
1993 European Arts Project.
1992 South West Arts writing workshops.
1986 BP Research Funding, Canada.
1983 South West Choreographic Award.

Contact: +44 (0)7 703 323 610

Wadiz

BA (Hons) Music (Sound & Image)

Currently appearing with his brother Amaz at The Hermitage in the Dorgonne & Maybrook musical *Above And Beyond.*

Martin Walker

BA (Hons) Wood Turner

Martin Walker is not well known as a founding father of research into relative humidity. In the early sixties, among many outstanding achievements in the field (adjacent to Hyderabad Racecourse), he won a local Egg 'n Sperm race, subsequently appearing in fancy dress in a privately funded developmental stage.

He found God during a childhood game of Hide 'n Seek (which didn't officially end) and although he may not know it, God has never needed to look for him.

Drawing on ancient Sufi texts in his teenage years lead to him being deported from Iraq, and the start of a semblance of a career as a graffiti artiste.

Late in 2008 (and most other years), he floated the idea of an unauthorised biographical ketch in the company of Andrew Sneeze, a previously lunched shipwright.

He now lives, parents, teaches and learns in England.

Francis Porter

BA (Hons) Graphic Design

Technical assistance.

www.francisporterdesign.com

For every copy sold, a donation goes to:

Trees For Health www.treesforhealth.org

An organisation of volunteers aiming to cultivate healthy communities and healthy ecosystems by revitalising our knowledge and use of woodland.

Moor Trees www.moortrees.org

A charity based in Devon, UK. We restore native woodland, grow local provenance trees in our community tree nurseries from locally collected seed, and run research, education and training programmes with partner schools, colleges and universities. Our aim is also social, so we build biodiversity by working with local people. As such, every year we work with hundreds of volunteers of all ages and abilities.

www.ingramcontent.com/pod-product-compliance
Lightning Source LLC
Chambersburg PA
CBHW051803040426
42446CB00007B/486